From the Small Bu............. r rimer Series

Small Business Financial Statements

What They Are, How to Understand Them, and How to Use Them

by

Bob Foster

Copyright Page

Contact:
bob@business-solutions-and-resources.com

Website:
www.business-solutions-and-resources.com

Table of Contents

Introduction

This book is one of the *Small Business Primer Series*, and is directed primarily at the aspiring entrepreneur and the new small business owner — those who have little experience or knowledge about business financial statements.

Small business financial statements are a key element in the successful operation of a small business. Yet, to many budding entrepreneurs, their use is a mystery. It is the intention of this book to remove that mystery and turn financial statements into a useful management tool for all small business owners — and about-to-become owners.

I want to make it clear here that I am *NOT* an accountant or a bookkeeper. I am a serial CEO and consultant to businesses in critical financial stress. I specialize in saving businesses deemed unsalvageable. *And financial statements are the most important tools in my business toolbox.*

Let me also say that this book is not an accounting book. It has been prepared specifically for small business owners and aspiring entrepreneurs so that they may understand the importance of financial statements, and how to utilize them in running their business more efficiently.

Additionally, the information presented in this book is not directed at those who want to understand financial statements for the purpose of investing in publicly traded stocks. Although anyone can learn the structure of financial statements from this book, there are many other factors to consider about a stock before an investment should be made.

We will begin to unravel the mystery of financial statements by discussing the importance of good accounting practices — the foster child of most startups and small businesses. Without proper bookkeeping and accounting oversight, financial statements can be worthless ... or worse!

The following chapters of this book will then deal with the basic concept of financial statements; what they are; how they are set up; how to understand them; and how to use them in running your business.

Most importantly, we will look at how you can quickly analyze the performance of your own business — or any other set of financial statements.

The latter chapters will deal with analyzing cash flow, auditing financial statements, preparing *Pro forma* financial statements and, what I call, "complementary" record keeping.

There are sample financial statements in the *Appendix* of this book, or you can download full-size pdf versions at:

Balance Sheet —

http://www.business-solutions-and-resources.com/support-files/sample-balance-sheet.pdf

Profit & Loss Statement —

http://www.business-solutions-and-resources.com/support-files/sample-p-and-l.pdf

These sample financial statements are referred to throughout this book.

This book is presented as a reference book that can be used indefinitely to answer questions about the complexities of business financial statements.

Accounting practices change very little over the years, so the information presented here is virtually timeless.

Small Business Accounting

Keeping accurate financial records is one of the most important functions of running a business … and yet, most small business owners give it short shrift.

Of all the troubled businesses I have looked at, I have never seen one that had a good accounting system in place, with up-to-date data and reports. Actually, good accounting may have kept them out of trouble all along.

If you are an entrepreneur starting your first business, I'll bet you have not given a lot of thought to your small business accounting (unless you are an accountant). Very few do, so you are not alone. And yet, it is one of the most important aspects of starting up and operating your small business.

Obviously, you want your invoices or billings to go out quickly, and accurately, with collections up to date, and money deposited in the bank as quickly as possible. You also want all the records that support these activities kept up to date.

Carefully controlling cash flow — both historically and projected — is critical, because one thing you never want to see is a stack of bills to pay and then be surprised that there is no money to pay them.

Of course, I don't even need to mention payroll—your employees need to be paid on time, every time.

Don't Stop There!

The above is usually about where most entrepreneurs stop thinking about accounting or bookkeeping. If you are working on a new startup, you likely think; "… financial reports are not of major concern at this point, and all the other financial details can be handled by a yet-to-be-hired bookkeeper"—*BIG MISTAKE!*

The day you spend your first dollar on your business is the day you should have your first bookkeeping system in place … no matter how simple it may be.

In addition to needing accurate financial information to run your business; if you ever decide to sell your business, or merge it with another, the due diligence process could go all the way back to the spending of that first dollar.

One thing to be aware of is that small business accounting systems do not need to be onerous. If you have a very small micro-business, with no employees, your system could be as simple as your sales and expense numbers jotted down in a notebook every day.

These numbers could then be summarized at the end of each month to determine your sales and profitability trends. This information, along with appropriate receipts, can then be used by your accountant to prepare tax returns at the end of the year.

As your business grows, the notebook accounting system will no longer suffice — that is when it is time to either outsource your bookkeeping, or bring in a part time bookkeeper.

The key is that whatever system, person, or service you use, it needs to be factual, accurate, and up-to-date — and not take a lot of your valuable time away from your business.

*NOTE: I will remind you that I am not an accountant and any suggestions I make are made from the viewpoint of a business owner/CEO/consultant. My remarks deal only with the **use** of accountant/bookkeeper-prepared records and reports. If you have any questions regarding the technicalities of bookkeeping or accounting, please refer them to your bookkeeper or accountant.*

Financial Statements

I have found that the thing most new entrepreneurs don't understand well is the standard financial information provided on their *Financial Statements*. If you are not clear on how financial statements are used; how they are created; how they can benefit you and your business; and how others view them; — you need to learn as quickly as possible.

I can't emphasize enough, the need for you to understand your financial statements, and how they should be used.

You also need to know how to analyze financial statements; what auditing financial statements means; how to build *Pro forma Financial Statements*; and what a *Cash Flow Analysis* is.

These and other aspects of small business accounting knowledge are absolutely mandatory for the small business entrepreneur to be successful today. You don't really need to know how to prepare financial statements, but you do need to know how to read and use them.

So, the following chapters of this book discuss all aspects of financial statements. This information should give you the knowledge you need to use financial statements as an important tool in running your business successfully.

Small Business Financial Statements

As I mentioned earlier, many business owners do not believe they need small business financial statements. As long as there is money in the bank to pay their bills they are happy. They just want to run their business, and not have to monkey with things like "bookkeeping."

If this describes you, it is highly unlikely you will see your business grow and become as successful as it could be. But even if it does become successful, you may someday want to borrow money from the bank for an expansion, and your banker will want to see several years worth of financial statements.

Or ... the day may come when you want to sell your business and the prospective buyer will want to see your historical financial statements, or....

The point is: You need, and will continue to need, a timely set of financial statements for your small business, especially as it grows and becomes more successful.

I want to emphasize here that you do not need to be a bookkeeper or accountant to read and understand your financial statements. All that is required is a general knowledge of financial statements — so let's start with...

What are Financial Statements — Exactly?

Small business financial statements are the summary reports on the operation of your business. Note that they are simply "reports" of what is contained in your accounting records — they are not where you do your bookkeeping. They are your "scorecard," and the "tally" of your business operations.

Financial statements are normally composed of three primary documents:

Balance Sheet

This is the section of financial statements that shows your *Assets* (the things your business owns, and what is owed to your business), and *Liabilities* (the things your business owes others).

Profit and Loss Statement (P&L)

This section shows how well your business performed during specified periods of time (as specified by you). It simply shows sales minus expenses equals profit (or loss).

Statement of Cash Flow

This section shows how cash comes into and flows out of your business. However, in very small businesses this report can be almost insignificant and is usually disregarded (there are better ways to analyze and control cash flow), while in larger small businesses this report can be much more complex — and valuable.

Note: In small businesses, the "retained earnings" information is included as a section of the *Balance Sheet,* while larger companies will often have a *Retained Earnings Statement* as a separate section of their financial statements.

For our purposes, the "retained earnings" information will be included in the *Balance Sheet,* as we'll discuss later.

Who Prepares Financial Statements?

For the simplest sole proprietorship of a micro-business, your "official" small business financial statements might simply be a copy of your annual tax return.

More than likely you can prepare this document yourself … or, you can have a bookkeeping service or tax preparer fill out your tax returns (which is what I recommend).

If your business is a bit larger, then you will likely need "official" financial statements. This is especially true if you are dealing with more complex issues like inventory, multiple product lines, depreciation, amortization, etc.

When you reach this stage of your business, I strongly recommend outsourcing your bookkeeping and the preparation of your financial statements.

Or, you can have a part-time bookkeeper come into your place of business to do your bookkeeping and prepare your small business financial statements.

The point here is that you, as the small business owner, at some point should not be involved in the day-to-day bookkeeping, nor in the "preparation" of your small business financial statements.

Understand your financial statements — yes! Analyze your financial statements — absolutely! Know how to use your financial statements — of course!

Just don't try to be your company's accountant when running your daily business consumes more and more of your time.

How Often Are Financial Statements Prepared?

Financial Statements are usually prepared monthly, or at least quarterly. It is most important that they be prepared at year-end for the entire year.

If you start your business in mid-year, then you will still want financial statements prepared at the end of the calendar year (assuming your fiscal year is the same as the calendar year).

This is when your accountant will prepare your tax returns, and everything "resets" to start a new year.

What Are Financial Statements Used For?

I am frequently questioned about the uses of financial statements, because they are not part of the "production" aspect of a business.

I have even had business owners tell me they didn't think they needed financial statements — they could just take their big box of receipts into their tax person once a year and that worked just fine ... and "look at all the money I'm saving."

This is usually the same business owner who also complains when the bank won't loan them any money, or some agency or creditor is demanding copies of their financial statements — and they don't have any.

Actually, there are many important uses of financial statements — if they are accurately prepared in a timely manner. Here are a few:

You need them on a regular basis as your report card on how your business is doing ... you need them to compare them to your Business planning.

Don't even think about going to your banker without a complete set of financial statements.

Your insurance company may want periodic copies of your financial statements.

Some of your suppliers will require a copy of your financial statements when you ask for credit terms.

For investors (if you have any), financial statements are the most important documents they want to see. This should also include your family and friends if they invested in your business.

If you operate an "open-books" business (and you should), your employees need to see your financial statements, or at least a summarized version of them.

When you go to sell your business, prospective buyers will want to see financial statements that can pass their due diligence.

Your tax preparer will want to see your financial statements when they prepare your tax returns, although your accountant will most likely be preparing both your financial statements and your tax returns.

Depending on your location, state and local taxing agencies may periodically want to see copies of your financial statements.

As you can see, there are many uses for financial statements that the startup entrepreneur may not be aware of initially. Let's just say it is best to start preparing regular financial statements as early as possible.

This has been a brief overview of small business financial statements, but there is much more information to cover, so I recommend you study the next few chapters carefully.

Sample Financial Statements

Sample financial statements are difficult to portray, because rarely do any two businesses have the same exact format for their statements.

Financial Statements for big corporations can reach book-size proportions — but that is not our interest here ... we want to learn what actual financial statements might look like for the newer entrepreneur with a startup business.

I want to emphasize that everything in this book is directed toward small business — incorporated or not. Understanding the financial statements of large publicly held companies is quite different and is not specifically addressed in this book (although the *concept* is the same).

We are going to review each of the primary documents that make up a set of financial statements, so we need something to look at and follow along as we dig into them.

As I mentioned earlier, I have created a simple set of sample financial statements. I created these financial documents for a fictitious company, *ABC Manufacturing, Inc.* and included them in the *Appendix* of this book.

In addition, I have provided a larger pdf copy of these same documents that can be downloaded and printed at:

18

Balance Sheet—

http://www.business-solutions-and-resources.com/support-files/sample-balance-sheet.pdf

Profit & Loss Statement—

http://www.business-solutions-and-resources.com/support-files/sample-p-and-l.pdf

These sample financial documents represent the most important accounting documents in your business. In this sample the *Balance Sheet* also contains the *Retained Earnings Statement* as a part of the Balance Sheet itself.

You will notice that I did ***not*** create a sample *Cash Flow Statement*, because frankly, I have found this document to not be a very good management tool for a small startup business—it is not timely enough. It is much more valuable as your business grows and your *Balance Sheet* becomes more robust.

When you are just starting a new business there are much better ways to monitor and control your cash.

If your business is even smaller (probably with no employees), you can prepare a much simpler set of financial statements than these samples. However, you will, at some point, require a proper set of financial statements—and, in my opinion, you should be using them for managing your business all along.

If you haven't done so yet, I recommend you review the sample financial statements in the *Appendix*, or better yet, download the pdf copies described previously.

I suggest you use them to follow along as we delve into the details of each document.

Since we are going to discuss each of these documents in some detail, I have created a separate chapter for each of them — following this chapter.

Balance Sheet

The *Balance Sheet* represents a picture of the financial health of your business at a given moment in time. In the example *Balance Sheet*, this "picture" was taken on December 31 of a fictitious year.

Typically, in a small business, financial statements arc prepared at the end of each month. This is not a hard and fast rule, but it is a good idea. If you space out your financial statements over a longer period, the information becomes out of date and of little use in helping you manage your business.

Quite often, the *Balance Sheet* will include a column for the prior year in addition to the current year, so that a comparison can be made between the years.

Format

The balance sheet is divided into three major sections; (1) *Assets* (the good stuff), (2) *Liabilities* (the not-so-good-stuff), and (3) *Stockholders Equity* (a record of all the money invested in your company — including all the profit your company has ever made).

The ***Assets*** section of your Balance Sheet is further divided into "Current Assets" and "Fixed Assets."

"Current Assets" are made up of cash and those things intended to be turned into cash in the reasonably near future—usually within the next 12 months.

"Fixed Assets" are property, plant, and equipment—those things not intended for sale and are used to manufacture or create the thing(s) you are selling.

Let's take a closer look at each of the detailed components of the *Balance Sheet*. It would be best if you could follow along with the example documents previously discussed:

Current Assets

Cash — This is your money in the bank and in your cash register. This can include savings accounts, marketable securities, and the like.

Accounts Receivable — This is money owed to your business for goods or services you provided to your customers. If you operate an all-cash business and you receive the money before you provide anything to your customers, you may not require this account at all.

Inventory — This represents all the money you have invested in inventory of materials or products and can include: raw materials, work in process, and finished products. Not all businesses have inventory.

Prepaid Expenses — There will likely be certain things you pay in advance, such as: rent, insurance premiums, leases, and the like. This is the account that holds those payments until the proper time to "expense" them.

Fixed Assets

Almost all fixed assets are depreciable, i.e., the value of the asset decreases with use. Your accountant will establish a "depreciation schedule" for your bookkeeper and the asset value shown on the *Balance Sheet* is always net of depreciation (sometimes your accountant will show the amount of depreciation as a separate line item).

Property — If your business owns any Real Estate this is where the value of that asset would be shown. Note that buildings are depreciated, while land is not.

Equipment — This component represents the value of any equipment your company owns, or is buying, that is used in the operation of your business. Sometimes office equipment is broken out separately, because it usually has a faster depreciation rate than factory equipment.

Vehicles — This is the total value of any vehicles your company owns, or is buying, and of course, is net of depreciation.

Total Assets

This is simply the sum of current assets plus fixed assets.

Now, for the other side of the Balance Sheet — *Liabilities*. The Liabilities section of your balance sheet is split between "Current Liabilities" (the things that should be paid soon), and "Long-term Liabilities,"

"Current Liabilities" are obligations that should be paid in the near future — no longer than the next 12 months.

"Long-term Liabilities" are obligations that extend beyond the next 12 months.

Here are the kinds of things that could appear in the Liabilities section of your Balance Sheet:

Current Liabilities

Revolving lines of credit — Many businesses set up a revolving line of credit with a bank as a form of operating capital. Sometimes money is borrowed against invoices and then the loan is paid down when the money is received from the customer. There are also other forms of revolving lines of credit however.

Accounts Payable — These are the bills you owe that must be paid relatively soon, depending on the terms of the account.

Current portion of long-term debt — This is the amount of the long-term debt that is to be paid during the current year.

Other — A business may have other forms of short-term debt that is to be paid within a short period of time, such as: a short-term equipment loan, or installment payments on a bulk shipment of inventory, and the like. Anything that does not fit in the above categories, but must be paid within 12 months.

Long-term Liabilities

Long-term debt — This category represents any loans or money that will be due and payable beyond the current year. This also includes "capital leases."

Loans payable to stockholders — When you or any other stockholder in your business loans money to your company, it is normally shown separately in this account on the Balance Sheet.

Other — Any other debt that is payable beyond the end of the current year.

Total Liabilities

The sum of "Current Liabilities" plus "Long-term Liabilities"

The third major section of your balance sheet is normally the *Stockholders Equity* section, and this is where understanding financial statements begins to get a little more complex.

This is where all your investment money is recorded. If you "loan" money to your business, it is shown in the *Liabilities* section (see above), but if you "invest" money in your business, it is shown in the *Stockholders Equity* section.

In addition, the *Stockholders Equity* section maintains a running record of the money your business has made since startup, and this is called **Retained Earnings**.

Let's look at the "Stockholder Equity" section in a little more detail:

Stockholders Equity

Common Stock — This is the value of the initial amount of money that was invested to start the company. If you are a sole proprietor without any stock involved, this line of your Balance Sheet would be called something your accountant sets up, such as "startup capital," or some such.

Paid-in Capital — This is the additional money you invested in your business after the initial investment. It is not uncommon to have an owner, or other stockholder, convert any loans they may have made to the business into "Paid-in Capital." This strengthens the Balance Sheet and raises the value of the business.

Retained Earnings-Cum — This is the amount of earnings your business has achieved in prior years. It is cumulative throughout the life of your business.

Retained Earnings-Current — This is the amount of profit your business has attained in the current year. The amount comes directly from the "Profit & Loss Statement." At the beginning of a new year this amount will be added to the "Retained Earnings-Cum."

The "Stockholders Equity" (investments) is added to "Retained Earnings" for a new total "Stockholders Equity" number.

In larger businesses, a separate report called the *Statement of Retained Earnings* is usually provided and it shows more detail about the money that makes up the "Retained Earnings" in the "Stockholders Equity" section of the Balance Sheet. This separate Retained Earnings document is especially important if your business pays dividends to stockholders.

For smaller businesses however, we can assume that the profit (or loss) for the period will simply be transferred over from the P&L to the *Stockholders Equity* section of the *Balance Sheet* as a bookkeeping entry called *"Retained Earnings Current Year."*

A special "Statement of Retained Earnings" is not required for most smaller businesses (although your accountant may not agree).

Total Liabilities and Stockholders Equity

Stockholders equity is added to the *Total Liabilities* number, which must equal the *Total Assets* number in order to have your Balance Sheet "balance."

After you begin to understand financial statements better, you will see that, the *Balance Sheet* is a snapshot record, or "tally" of the health and worth of your business — according to your accounting records.

You have "Assets" (what your company owns, or is owed by others), "Liabilities" (everything your company owes to someone else), and "Equity" (everything the owners or stockholders have invested in your company, plus profits to date).

The *Balance Sheet* is the most important accounting document for displaying the value of your business at any given time.

Profit and Loss (P&L) Statement

The *P&L Statement* is a record of the money your business received (Sales Revenue) during a specified period of time; the money your business spent (Expenses) during the same period; and the amount of profit (or loss) earned during the same period (revenue minus expenses).

This document can be quite simple for the smaller business … or extremely complex for big corporations. However, the basic concept and general format are always the same.

Please note that the P&L is not quite as cut-and-dried as the Balance Sheet. Your accountant will make suggestions on how to set up your P&L, depending on the nature of your business.

For some industries, standard formats have been developed. This helps to accurately compare your business to your industry standard and helps in understanding financial statements specifically for your industry. Your accountant should know about these common formats and will recommend the precise format for you.

Most importantly, you need a format that helps you analyze your own business.

Again, I would suggest you refer to the *Sample Profit and Loss Statement* we discussed earlier, so you can follow along with this discussion. This will help considerably in understanding financial statements as we proceed.

Profit & Loss Statements

This is the second document of your financial statements. Although the formatting of P&L Statements may vary from business to business (see above), they all have major components in common, as follows:

Sales — This is usually the money you receive for selling your product(s) or service(s), minus any "Returns or Allowances." This provides a *Net Sales* figure.

Cost of Sales — This is what you paid to acquire or produce your product(s) or service(s). If you are a one-person professional service, you may, or may not have an actual cost of sales. This section of the P&L can also get a little more complex if you have a manufacturing business and want to show inventories, purchases, and production labor in this section of the P&L (see example P&L).

The objective here is to arrive at a true cost of sales and at the same time track inventory levels, purchases, and production labor trends against sales. Although this is a common practice, it is not necessary for any business that does not carry an inventory of parts and/or products.

Gross Profit — This is simply "Net Sales" minus "Cost of Sales." This is the profit your business makes before any of your selling and administrative overhead costs are figured in.

Selling Expense — This is the expense incurred for selling whatever you are selling. It could be the cost of maintaining a sales staff, paying commissions, advertising, P.R., other forms of marketing, and any cost associated with the process of selling.

Some accountants will want to put this cost in as part of the Cost of Sales; some will put it as a separate standalone section below the Gross Profit line, and others will include it in with the General Operating Expenses.

Much depends on your accountant, your bookkeeping system, and the type of business you have — plus your own personal preference.

However, I always like to see it spelled out separately below the Gross Profit line.

Operating Expense — This is generally referred to as "overhead," and includes all the other expenses you incur in running your business, such as: wages, rent, utilities, communications, office supplies, etc. I prefer not to include depreciation, amortization, or interest in this section because they are more "strategic" expenses than the day-to-day cost of running your business.

31

This, of course, may disturb your accountant greatly because they usually like to show all expenses together. Accountants often have a difficult time understanding financial statements from a CEO's point of view.

Note: When accountants prepare your financial statements at year end, they will usually collapse these detailed line items of expense and show them as simply Selling, General and Administrative, or *S,G & A* expense. They may then show the details in the "Notes" section of their report. The sample P&L Statement in the *Appendix* shows an "expanded" version to better help in understanding P&L statements.

Operating Profit — EBITDA — EBITDA stands for *Earnings Before Interest, Taxes, Depreciation, and Amortization.* True Operating Profit (or EBITDA) is calculated by subtracting Selling Expense and Operating Expense (excluding interest, taxes, depreciation, and amortization) from Gross Profit.

This is a true measure of how your business operated during the specified period, because the numbers are not skewed by non-operating expenses such as: interest, taxes, depreciation, and amortization.

EBITDA is a number you and your bookkeeper will have to work on, because your accounting firm (if you have one) will likely pitch a fit when you ask them to do it.

EBITDA is more of an "operational" approach to your P&L, and less of an "accounting" approach.

Other Income (Expense) — You do have to account for all income and expense for your business, so this is where you would put non-operational items, such as: interest from bank accounts, tax refunds, miscellaneous income, etc. — as well as "strategic" expenses, such as: interest, depreciation, amortization, and the like. At least this is where I put all non-operational items even though many accountants disagree.

Pre-tax Profit — This is simply the total taxable profit your business made before paying income taxes, and is calculated by adding "Total Other Income (Expense)" to your *EBITDA Operating Profit.*

Income Tax Allowance — This is the total tax (including state income tax) you will be expected to pay on the profits from your business. Since most tax returns are prepared differently than P&L Statements are, the number here may not compare exactly with the tax number being shown on your tax returns.

Net Profit — This is the number that is usually referred to as "the bottom line," and normally the one you want to be as large as possible.

If you are going to do any serious analysis of your financials, you will need to work with an expanded P&L that shows much more detail than an accountant's more formal (summary) P&L.

With an expanded P&L you can make your own analysis of performance, determine the trends of certain line items, and if anything looks out of the ordinary, or questionable, you can request an "account analysis" from your bookkeeper.

When presenting your P&L to outsiders (banks, vendors, investors, etc.) you can collapse the format and eliminate much of the detail that likely would not mean much to those people anyway.

Statement of Cash Flow.

This is generally the third document of your set of Financial Statements. This document is usually prepared by your accountant, and is an integral part of your year-end financial statements—but usually not your interim statements.

It is valuable from the standpoint of telling you where you spent your cash during the last year, but it is not very helpful in running your business on a daily basis—there are better ways to do that.

This document can also be valuable for comparing your cash flows from year to year.

It is also an important document when discussing your business with bankers, stockholders, Venture Capitalists, and potential buyers of your business.

For daily operating information however, there are better ways to monitor your cash, so don't get too hung up on this document unless it is requested by outside sources.

In fact, in my opinion, for the small business, a "Statement of Cash Flow" document can be ignored all together—until your business becomes large enough that it becomes important to investors or buyers.

That is why I have not included a sample copy in either the Appendix, or the pdf download. If your accountant provides one at year-end, ask them to explain it to you, but don't worry about it if you don't really understand it.

However, *Cash Flow Analysis* and control is extremely important and I have briefly discussed this in a later chapter.

Financial Statement Analysis

Financial statement analysis is, of course, the underlying purpose of preparing financial statements. Everyone who looks at your financial statements will be automatically performing some form of analysis.

Your banker will analyze your financial statements to determine your capability of paying back a loan.

Your investor(s) will always perform a financial statement analysis to determine if you have been performing according to plan, and/or whether your business is a good investment.

Your suppliers will analyze your financial statements to determine your credit worthiness – and so on.

The point is: everyone who looks at your financial statements will conduct a financial statement analysis, in one form or another. That is why your documents need to be as accurate and truthful as possible.

You, as well as your business, will be judged according to your financial statements.

But the most important aspect of financial statement analysis is the analysis you perform yourself.

There are three major analyses you need to make. There are many others as well, but we'll stick to the three major ones for now, as follows:

Actual vs. Planned Performance

You did considerable business planning (at least you should have) before you started your business—and you likely updated it for banks, investors, or suppliers—complete with Pro forma financial statements (more on Pro forma statements later).

So, after your business is operating, you will need to compare your actual performance (from your financial statements) against your planned performance (from your pro forma financial statements).

This financial statement analysis should be performed line item by line item. If you had fewer sales than planned … you should know or find out why. If any costs were greater than planned … again, you should know or find out why.

Every dollar received, and every dollar spent shows up on your financial statements, and every dollar that is different than you planned should be analyzed. This can be extremely valuable, as this analysis can tell you where you may need to modify your planning—or how you need to change the running of your business.

This is where it becomes important to have an advisory group where you can bounce information, and ideas, around.

Trend Analysis

By comparing current financial statements to previous financial statements you can see which areas of your business have changed, and by how much. Then you need to determine why the change occurred, whether positive or negative.

Are sales trending up? Are costs trending down (and which ones aren't)? Are profits trending up? Is your cash flow improving? These are the types of things you will want to look at in your financial statement analysis.

Like the performance analysis, you need to analyze your financial statements line item by line item to determine trends ... and don't be afraid to change your planning (or your operations) if you see a new trend emerging.

Industry Standards Comparison—Ratios

This analysis is not only a comparison of your business's performance to others in your industry, but also to standards set by your banker, your investor(s), your advisory group, or yourself.

These comparisons are usually made in the form of financial "ratios." Here are a few of the more common financial ratio analyses:

Balance Sheet Ratios.

Balance Sheet ratios typically measure the strength of your business, using the following formulas:

Current Ratio — This is one of the most widely used tests of financial strength, and is calculated by dividing Current Assets by Current Liabilities. This ratio is used to determine if your business is likely to be able to pay its bills.

Obviously, a minimum acceptable ratio would be 1:1; otherwise your company would not be expected to pay its bills on time. A ratio of 2:1 is much more acceptable, and the higher, the better.

Quick Ratio — This is sometimes called the "acid test" ratio because it concentrates on only the more liquid assets of your business. It is calculated by dividing the sum of Cash and Receivables by Current Liabilities. It excludes inventories or any other current asset that might have questionable liquidity. Depending on your history for collecting receivables, a satisfactory ratio is 1:1.

Working Capital — Bankers especially, watch this calculation very closely as it deals more with cash flow than just a simple ratio. Working Capital equals Current Assets minus Current Liabilities. Quite often your banker will tie your loan approval amount to a minimum Working Capital requirement.

Inventory Turnover Ratio — Not every business has an inventory that needs to be of concern, and if that is your situation you can ignore this ratio. However, if you are concerned about your inventory, then you definitely should watch this ratio carefully when comparing it to industry guidelines.

This ratio tells you if your inventory is turning over fast enough, and is usually calculated by dividing Net Sales by your average Inventory (at cost).

It is also sometimes calculated by dividing Cost of Sales by your average Inventory (at cost). It usually depends on how your industry generally calculates this ratio.

Ask your accountant for your specific industry guidelines.

Leverage Ratio — This is another of the analyses used by bankers to determine if your business is credit worthy. It basically shows the extent your business relies on debt to keep operating and is calculated by dividing Total Liabilities by Net Worth (total assets minus total liabilities).

Obviously, the higher the ratio is, the more risky it becomes to extend credit to your business. This is often the calculation a supplier to your business will make before extending credit to you.

41

****

P&L Ratios

Profit and Loss (P&L) documents also have some important ratio calculations for your financial statement analysis:

Gross Profit Ratio — This is the most common calculation on your P&L — it is simply your Gross Profit divided by Net Sales. Often, different industries will have standard guidelines that you can compare your business's numbers to. It is also desirable to watch your trends and not let this number drop below your target.

Line Item Trends — You will want to look at each line item on your P&L and determine if it is trending in the right direction from prior P&Ls. Are sales and profits going up, and are expenses trending down?

Whenever you have an undesirable trend, you need to determine why and make corrections accordingly. This also must be done in a very timely manner — otherwise, you will soon find yourself up the creek without a paddle.

Net Profit Ratio — This calculation is simply Net Pre-tax Profit divided by Net Sales. Other than wanting this number to be as large as possible, I usually don't pay too much attention to it because it includes too many non-operating costs (depreciation, amortization, etc.) to be of any real analytic value. (Your banker, or investor, will be interested however.)

Management Ratios.

There are a couple of other ratios that interested outside parties may want to analyze:

Return on Assets — This is calculated by dividing Net Pre-tax Profit by Total Assets. The ratio is supposed to indicate how efficiently you are utilizing your assets. To me this is a useless analysis for helping you run your business, however, bankers and investors will always calculate this ratio if you don't.

Return on Investment (ROI) — To a bank or investor this is a very important ratio. It is supposed to tell you — the business owner — if you are investing your time, and money, properly, or should you just liquidate your business and put the money into a savings account. As an entrepreneur, this idea should never enter your mind — it is a thought only to be discussed by academics and bankers.

However, if you do want this information, I recommend you discuss this calculation with your accountant, because the formula is sometimes different for sole proprietorships and LLCs, than for corporations. If your bank needs this information, they usually use their own formula anyway.

Don't worry about needing to learn all the technicalities of financial statement analysis — there are many sources of expert help and it would not be time consuming nor costly to have your accountant or a member of your advisory board assist you until you get the hang of it.

The following chapter is basically an exhibit of how a person might analyze the sample financial statements shown in the *Appendix,* or the downloaded pdf statements.

Example of Financial Statement Analysis

There are times when you may need to do a quick analysis of a business's *Financial Statements*. Perhaps you are looking for a business to buy; or you are in an advisory capacity and are asked your opinion on the health of a business; or the business is in trouble and the owner would like some direction on how to turn it around.

One of the key issues to look at is how the money has been spent or invested, and what is the condition of cash and the potential for converting assets to cash.

If you were buying the business, or the business needed to be turned around, the operation would be changed anyway, so cash becomes the biggest issue in these cases.

Here is the procedure I usually use for taking a first pass through a business's financial statements to determine if they warrant any additional analysis time.

We will use the sample financial statements included in the *Appendix*, or that you previously downloaded, and I will provide a comment under the title of *Analysis* for each item discussed on our sample financial statement. This way you can follow along as we analyze the statement:

Balance Sheet

Assets

Current Assets

Cash — Start with the Balance Sheet and look at *Cash* first. Does the business have enough cash to operate in the short term (a day, a week or a month)? Is there money in savings, or some securities that can be easily liquidated?

> *Analysis:* Our sample business has a reasonable cash balance on hand for the size of the business. However, it would be better if there were some easily liquidated securities showing.

Accounts Receivable — Look at *Accounts Receivable* (A/R). Does the amount seem fairly normal for the size of business? Make a note to ask for an "Aged A/R Report." It is important to determine what the quality of the customer accounts are, and whether they are being actively overseen.

> *Analysis:* This all depends on the aging of the accounts and the practices of the business. The amount shown appears o.k. for this first pass through. Be sure to review the aged A/R report however, to determine if there are any uncollectable accounts included.

Inventory — If there is *Inventory* involved, check to see if it appears to be about the right size for the size of business. Make a quick calculation of inventory turnover. Make a note to check the business's inventory control system and possibly make a few random counts of your own — if appropriate. Inventory can be a key issue in many businesses, so this is an area that needs careful study.

> *Analysis:* At first glance this item does not appear out of line, but inventory is always an area that requires more careful analysis. A random search for obsolescence is always desirable, and you should be aware that inventory numbers are *never* accurate.

Total Current Assets — Quickly view the remaining *Current Assets* and see if you can spot any item that seems out of the ordinary. Is there a large amount of "Prepaid Expenses?" Are there any notable assets that can be turned into cash if needed?

> *Analysis:* For this quite small company, the Current Assets seem to be satisfactory.

Fixed Assets — Look at *Fixed Assets* and consider if there is anything that appears at first glance that is out of line. Could any of these line items be converted to cash if needed? Could property be borrowed against; could equipment or vehicles be sold and leased back; is there anything else of value that could be converted to cash?

> *Analysis:* For our sample business, *Equipment and Vehicles* appear to be in line, but a note should be made to check

further into the "Property" category. This may be an area for future cash generation—if needed.

Liabilities

Current Liabilities

Lines of Credit—Review any short-term debts or revolving lines of credit to see if payments are current. Make a note to review any contracts or agreements for payment terms.

> *Analysis:* Assuming all payment terms are being met, this area of the Balance Sheet looks o.k.

Accounts Payable—Look especially at the "Aged Accounts Payable (A/P) Report." This should be available from the bookkeeper. If the business is behind on their A/P payments, you will want a good explanation for the reason.

> *Analysis:* Assuming the A/P payments are all current, this looks like an acceptable A/P balance.

Current Portion of Long-term Debt—This should be the portion of the long-term debt that is being paid off this year. Check this number against the long-term debt number to see if it appears reasonable.

> *Analysis:* Since this number should reduce each month, the number shown depends on how far into the year the statement is. However, it is always advisable to inquire about how the number was determined.

Long-term Liabilities

Long-term Debt — Review all long-term financial agreements, including leases. Are all payments current? Is the total debt in line with the size of the business, or is the long-term debt an anchor that could hold the business back from succeeding? Look at all the contracts to make sure they were executed properly.

> *Analysis:* This category does not seem to be out of line, but further analysis should be made on the interest rates for the long-term debt vs. the revolving lines of credit, to see if an increase in long-term debt to pay off the short-term debt could reduce the amount being paid in interest.

Loans Payable to Stockholders — Many small businesses borrow money from their owner(s). This line item is where that loan balance would be shown. Be sure to check to see if there is a formal document with terms for any loans, and what the status is on the payments.

> *Analysis:* The "Loans Payable to Stockholders" will need to be more closely reviewed. What is the agreement on this loan, and is there a legal contract for the loan? Are payments being made on this loan?

Stockholders Equity and Retained Earnings

Common Stock — This is the amount of money originally invested in the business to get it started. It can be called different things depending on the legal organization of the business. If you were buying this business, this is an item you would analyze in your "Due Diligence" study.

Additional Paid-in Capital — This is money that was paid in after the business was formed. For small businesses it is not uncommon for a debt holder to convert their loan in exchange for stock, and that transaction would show up here. This is also an item you would analyze during your "Due Diligence."

Retained Earnings from Prior years — This is a record of all the profit (and loss) the business has accumulated since it started up. It is a cumulative number for all the years up to the present, but not from the current year. You would want to compare the cumulative profit from each reporting period statement to this number — they should be identical … but often are not.

> *Analysis:* Since this number includes profits accumulated from the start of business, the rating of the number obviously depends on how long the business has been in operation. If the business has been operating for a number of years, and the retained earnings are low, that means the business has not done well in past years. The reason needs to be researched.

Retained Earnings from Current P&L — This is the sum total of all the profit (and loss) for the months of the current year. This number should be the sum of each P&L that has been produced so far this year. It sounds simple, but it seems that there is often a major problem in getting this number on the Balance Sheet to be the same as the cumulative number on the P&L. If they don't match, it will require more analysis.

> *Analysis:* It has always amazed me that so many financial statements have different numbers on the Balance Sheet and the P&L statement in this category. In our example statements, the numbers are the same. Make sure any financial statements you analyze also match.

Total Stockholders Equity — This number represents all the money that was ever invested in the business, *plus*, all the money the business has earned since it started up. This is the sum total that the owner(s) have invested and earned. When added to the *Liabilities*, the new number should be the same as the *Total Assets* — in order for the *Balance Sheet* to "Balance."

> *Analysis:* The "Stockholders Equity" category seems to be o.k. A quick analysis of the current "Retained Earnings" number vs. the cumulative year-to-date profit on the individual P&L statements should be made however.

****

Just by reviewing the *Balance Sheet* you now know whether you are looking at a healthy business, or one that is not so healthy — maybe dying.

You should also have a pretty good idea about how additional cash could be extracted out of the Assets, and what might be done about reducing, or improving, the Liabilities.

The next step is to look at the *Profit & Loss (P&L) Statement* to see how the business has been run, and how it might be changed to turn it around and/or make it more successful.

Let's start at the top and work our way down. Be sure to refer to the sample *P&L* as we review the various line items:

Profit & Loss (P&L)

The P&L is usually not quite as standardized as the Balance Sheet. The format is only generally the same between businesses, and your accountant usually sets the exact form. We will follow the format that appears in the *Appendix* of this book, or that you previously downloaded, so follow along as we discuss each of the line items:

Sales

This is the total Gross Sales, or Revenue, that the business received during the bookkeeping period, usually a calendar month.

Analysis: This number is usually compared to both a forecast and the previous months to determine performance against expectations. This is also the number that all other entries on the P&L are compared to — see percentages.

Returns and Allowances — This number represents any returns by customers, or discounts that were given customers. There is usually a nominal percentage for this number. For an analysis, check to see that the amount does not vary significantly from any standard or average for the industry.

Analysis: The small amount shown appears to be o.k.

Cost of Sales

Inventory — The financial statements that you might analyze may not have any inventory, but in the event it does, it can be shown in a variety of ways.

Many books have been written about Inventory, so we won't go into much detail here. In the sample P&L, I have shown Beginning Inventory, Purchases (of either raw material, parts, or finished product), Production Labor (that was used to transform any raw material or parts into finished product), and then the Ending Inventory.

The beginning inventory is added to the purchases and the production labor; then the ending inventory is subtracted from this total to leave the business with a number for the

Cost of Sales. This is the basic concept of how the cost of material used in production is calculated — but there are many ways to depict the actual numbers on the P&L. You may need some explanation from your accountant to help in this area.

> *Analysis:* The *Cost of Sales* number in our sample P&L seems to be quite high. This could be because of the products being made, or any non-production costs the accountant put into this category, in which case the numbers may be o.k. But it is an area that definitely needs additional analysis.

Gross Profit

This is simply the *Sales* minus the *Cost of Sales.*

> *Analysis:* The *Gross Profit* in the sample P&L appears to be too low. It normally should be higher than this in a small manufacturing company. However, this particular business might categorize their expenses so that some overhead expenses are included in the *Cost of Sales.* That is why this line item will need additional analysis.

Selling Expense

This expense is often combined with general overhead operating expense, but some accountants prefer to break it out separately to show exactly how much it costs the business to market and sell their product or service. I prefer the latter form.

Some industries provide standard guidelines for what percentage this Selling Expense should be. Your accountant can give you the guideline for your particular industry.

> *Analysis:* This business has a *Selling Expense* of 7.2%, which could be considered acceptable if the expense is creating fast growth in Sales. Some industries, especially high-tech companies, consider a much higher number to be acceptable.

Operating Expense

This category of expense includes the administrative overhead costs required to run the business. Things like salaries (other than production and selling), payroll taxes and benefits, office supplies, utilities, rent, and the like. It should not include interest, depreciation, or amortization charges however.

> *Analysis:* This is an area that can quickly get out of control. An expense percentage of 16.4% might be considered high in some industries, so the large "salaries" category of expense in our sample P&L is a place that needs more analysis.

Operating Profit — EBITDA

EBITDA stands for *Earnings Before Interest, Taxes Depreciation, and Amortization.* This is the number that tells you how well you are running your business on a day-to-day basis.

Analysis. Our sample business shows an EBITDA of 16.4%. This might be considered o.k. but it certainly leaves room for improvement. It does provide something to build on however.

Other Income (Expense)

Interest — This category of expense would include the interest paid on the debt of the business. Any interest collected on A/R accounts, bank accounts, investments, etc. would also be shown here as *income*.

> *Analysis:* Our sample P&L shows only interest *Expense*, so a note should be made to inquire about any interest, or other, income.

Depreciation — The accountant for this company will prepare a "depreciation schedule" that shows the amount of depreciation on all the depreciable assets. The depreciation schedule normally shows monthly amounts that can be entered by your bookkeeper. Depreciation for the entire year is always reviewed by your accountant at year-end and adjusted if necessary.

Or, in a business this small, depreciation and amortization might only be added by your accountant at year-end.

> *Analysis:* Depreciation does have a direct bearing on the tax liability of the business, so you would want to ascertain how much remaining depreciation is available for the future.

Amortization — This category, like depreciation, is a part of the accountant's world. It is expense put aside to reduce the cost of a non-depreciable asset. It may include such things as loan fees, goodwill, and the like.

Analysis: Amortization also has a bearing on the tax liability of the business, so this is an area that should be further studied for future tax benefits.

Income Tax Allowance — This is usually only a rough estimate and is a combination of state and federal taxes. Some states have different types of taxes on a business, so this number is usually not very accurate until an accountant completes their year-end tax work.

Analysis: Hard to analyze other than to check to see whether or not the number on the P&L was prepared by an accountant for the date of the statement.

Net Profit

This is the number that most people look at first — although I am usually more interested in the EBITDA number. Net Profit is the final result from all the machinations of running a small business.

Analysis: Many people might consider the Net Profit of 8.3% (of Sales) on our example to be low. But in a small closely held business, tax liability is always a consideration, so in some cases, it is better to have this number be quite low. This is where you would want to meet with the company's accountant to discuss this issue.

****

If you decide after this first quick analysis that the business is worth a further look, you can next apply the ratio analyses presented in the prior chapter.

These ratios usually won't give you the direct information you need to make any decisions about the business, but they certainly do direct you as to where to concentrate on doing further deep investigation.

All through this process you should be making lists of questions for the owner(s) and/or management. It is important that you get all your questions answered to you satisfaction. Otherwise, it would be best to walk away from any deal, or, if you are an advisor, tell them you cannot help them until your questions are answered.

You must have backup information to the numbers on financial statements when you are doing a detailed analysis.

In the event you determine that the business is beyond help, be sure to tell them to prepare for a shutdown — and if they need any guidance with that they should consult this URL, http://www.business-solutions-and-resources.com/closing-a-business.html

Well, that is the procedure I use for an initial review and analysis of small business financial statements. The financial statement is like a "portal," or entry into the workings of a business, and if you decide to look deeper into the business, it can serve as a roadmap showing you where to look.

The more financial statements you look at and analyze, the better you will become at analyzing them, so it would be good practice to review as many as you can.

Just remember that large public corporations are not this easy to analyze and if you are making an analysis for stock investment purposes there are many books out there that can help you make your decisions.

The next thing you should consider, regarding your own financial statements, is the auditing process, because your banker or investor(s) will likely require an "audit" at some point. The next chapter discusses *Auditing Financial Statements*.

Auditing Financial Statements

Auditing financial statements is something most new entrepreneurs will not have to think about for a long time — if ever.

Even a successful and growing small business should not be alarmed when a third-party — banker, investor, creditor, buyer, etc. — asks for "audited" financial statements, because that is rarely what they are actually asking for.

What these third-parties really want to see is some assurance that the financial statements provided by a business, are reasonably accurate and are likely free of any major oversight, or material errors. The term "audit" when used in the small business community is similar to the use of the term "kleenex" when a person simply wants a facial tissue. *(Note: It is likely that your accountant will strongly disagree with this analogy).*

Any third-party dealing with newer small businesses is well aware that actually "auditing" financial statements is cost prohibitive for these young businesses. Requiring a small business to pay for a true "audit" could put many of them out of business.

Of the 25+ million businesses that have started up over the last 4 years (*Kauffman Foundation* data), only a very few will ever be required to provide "audited" financial statements—even when asked.

However, when you do grow your business to the point of needing to more heavily involve outsiders (bankers, investors, etc.), you will likely need to provide some level of assurance that your financial statements are reasonably accurate.

So, let's take a look at the various levels of "assurance" that you may be asked to provide as your business continues to grow.

Levels of Assurance

There are 5 primary levels of assurance that are typically provided to interested parties outside your business. These are discussed below. Just be aware that you will need to discuss the specific needs of your own business with your accountant before starting any of these activities:

Internally Prepared Financial Statements

These are the regular financial statements that you, or your bookkeeper, prepare in the normal course of business. Usually you will be asked to provide last year's year-end financial statements, plus current year-to-date statements.

In most cases, a third party will also want to see a copy of your business's last-year's tax return. The comparison of the tax return to the financial statements will give the third-party the minimum assurance they may need at that time.

For the young small business, involving minimum third-party participation, this is usually all that is required to provide adequate assurances of financial status — when asked.

Compilation

This level of assurance is where your outside accountant (CPA or CA) takes the financial information you provide, and "compiles" it into proper financial statement form.

Your accountant will also provide a cover letter with the compiled statements saying that they did not audit the information, and that they do not offer any assurances on the accuracy of the numbers presented. The "compilation" only assures the third-party that the "presentation" of the numbers is correct — with no assurance on the numbers themselves.

This form of accountant-prepared financial statements is the least expensive, and is usually used when the business does not have the capability to generate internally prepared financial statements. Also, this will usually only work for the very smallest, or very new business.

(Note: There is a caveat to your accountant's responsibility when preparing a "compilation." This regards inaccurate, incomplete, or misleading information ... or obvious departure from Generally Accepted Accounting Principles. *Discuss this with your accountant before starting a compilation).*

Review

This is the most common form of assurance of financial statements accuracy for small businesses. First of all, it is not an audit—it is much less extensive. The objective of the "review" is for your outside accountant (CPA or CA) to provide limited assurance that your financial statements are basically in conformity with *Generally Accepted Accounting Principles* (GAAP).

Your outside accountant will assess management's representations, and focus more on the relationships of accounting information rather than the verification of the company's numbers. Your accountant will write a cover letter with the Review document stating that they performed a "review," not an "audit."

This level of assurance of financial statements accuracy is widely used in small business, and is usually adequate for nearly all small business requirements. Unless there is a suspicion of fraud or substantial errors, there is usually no need to go beyond this level.

Review with Observed Inventory

For some companies with large, complex, or expensive, inventories, a standard "Review" may not be acceptable to everyone. In this case, your outside accountant will come on-site to participate in ("observe") the taking of your physical inventory. They will randomly recount several of your inventory items and then express an opinion on the accuracy of your inventory.

This is quite a bit more expensive than a simple Review, but far less costly than a complete "audit." If you have a substantial investment in inventory, your bank, or investors, will often request this additional step.

Audit

This is what is usually thought of when the term "auditing financial statements" is mentioned. However, it is rarely needed for newer small businesses, unless you are trying to sell, or merge, your business. Then the buyers will sometimes require "audited" financial statements.

Also, as your business matures and grows, you may need to provide audited financial statements to your financial institution, or investors.

In an audit, your accountant will perform substantial analysis of your financial information, gather additional information from management, and verify certain information through contacts external to the business. An audit is a complex investigation and analysis of your financial records, including the general operating practices of your business.

This is always an expensive project, so do not approach it lightly, and do not do it unless you absolutely have to.

Remember, you are a small business, not a public corporation, and your level of assurance only needs to satisfy those few people who require some form of assurance of the accuracy of your financial statements.

So, don't spend money on "auditing" financial statements until you are forced to, and don't provide a higher level of assurance than is absolutely required.

Selecting a CPA

Large publicly held corporations in the U.S. usually use one of the large national CPA firms to prepare their audited financial statements, but that is neither necessary nor desirable for your small company.

You can select a local or regional accounting firm, but, when you select your outside accountant, be sure to select one who can also prepare "audited" financial statements should that ever be required in the future.

If your accountant is already familiar with your operation and your accounting system, it often cuts down on the cost of performing a formal audit. Usually a local CPA firm is perfectly capable of doing this.

If you are just starting up, you do not need to worry about auditing financial statements just yet — that may come in the natural course of growing your business. Actually, you may never need a formal "audit" of your business's financial operations and statements.

However, in the process of doing your pre-venture planning it will become absolutely mandatory to prepare (and maintain) *Pro forma Financial Statements* for you to use as your road map.

Also, if you ever need to prepare a formal business plan, you will need to include *Pro forma Financial Statements* in that document.

So, let's take a look at these statements in the next chapter.

Pro forma Financial Statements

Check out "pro forma financial statements" in Wikipedia and you will find five different definitions for the term. Interestingly, the "accounting" definition they provide is NOT the definition we are interested in here.

Wikipedia's "accounting" definition deals with the arcane calculation of profits and losses used to circumvent *Generally Accepted Accounting Principles* (GAAP), and has nothing to do with pro forma financial statements as we will use them.

As small business owners, we are only interested in a small business definition of pro forma financial statements, which can be simply stated as: *the anticipated financial statements resulting from future business transactions.*

Pro forma financial statements are basically a set of forecasts of what you think your financial statements will look like at a specified point in the future.

Format

Pro forma financial statements look exactly like regular, or actual, financial statements (or what your actual statements *will* look like if you are just starting up).

The only difference is that pro forma statements use your best estimate of future financial performance numbers instead of actual historical numbers from your bookkeeping system.

You will have at least two of the three elements of financial statements in your pro forma statements:

Balance Sheet (Retained Earnings will be included in the Balance Sheet)

Profit and Loss Statement (P&L)

Using Pro forma Statements

When you start building your dream plan, you will want to know how economically feasible your business idea is, so you will begin developing a set of pro forma statements – no matter how crude.

You will begin with what you think your sales might be, and what your costs might be. You then periodically modify these numbers as your business planning moves forward.

As you continually learn more about your market and you do more research, you will obviously update your sales estimates.

You will also determine more costs as you proceed, and you will want to update your forecasted expenses accordingly. That means you can use your pro forma statements as a "running record" of building your future business on paper.

If you have an investor or financial institution involved, you will need to formally format a complete set of Pro forma financial statements for your formal business plan.

This would be for presentations to your investor(s), or bank, etc. They will want to see what you believe your business is capable of doing in future months and years.

If you do not involve investors, or banks, you won't need to write a "formal" business plan, but you will always need to keep up your "planning," and updating your Pro forma financial statements.

Cash Flow Analysis

The cash flow analysis discussed here differs substantially from the *Statement of Cash Flow* included in formal financial statements. Instead of just reporting historical cash events, this analysis is composed primarily of your best detailed projections of what your business will need for future cash in the shorter term, and how you intend to spend that cash each month.

You then overlay actual cash in and cash out to see how close you came to your projections, and then modify your projections if necessary.

The most important use of a *Cash Flow Analysis* like this is to know in advance how much cash you will likely need tomorrow and in the short term, so unexpected expenses will never surprise you.

Since this document is not something most accountants work with, you will likely have to prepare it yourself until your business grows enough to support a qualified bookkeeper you can train to maintain it.

At the same time this document does not have to be overly formal or onerous.

I suggest making a simple EXCEL (or even handwritten) spreadsheet of fourteen columns. The first column depicts the line item names for *Receipts* (cash in) and *Expenses* (cash out).

The next 12 columns are simply one column per month for the next 12 months. The last column is simply the total of the 12-month projections so they can be crosschecked with the pro forma statements in your business planning.

I have prepared an example *Cash Flow Analysis* and included it in the *Appendix*. Or, you can also download a free pdf copy of an example form at this URL, http://www.business-solutions-and-resources.com/support-files/cash-flow-analysis.pdf

There is no blank worksheet provided, because no two businesses are similar enough to use a standard form. However, you can use the example form as a general model for your own worksheet.

I suggest you use the example form to follow along with the descriptions and explanations below of how to best use a similar form for your particular business:

Beginning Cash

This first line item is the amount of cash you have, or think you will have, at the beginning of the first month of your analysis.

Sales Billings

The next line item is the projected billings, or invoices you think you will be sending out to your customers for those sales you offer terms on. This can be taken directly from your pro forma P&L, but here, this line of numbers is for reference only, because for this analysis you cannot count your "cash" until you expect to actually receive it.

Sales Receipts

The third line item is the amount of money you expect to *collect* each month from your billings, and/or cash sales. It is assumed in this example that you offer terms to your customers so that collections will come sometime after your billings. A few customers may pay early; many will likely pay as agreed, while a number of them will pay late (in this example).

The point is: That collections always lag billings, and that is what comprises the financial term of "Accounts Receivable" (A/R) that you have on your Balance Sheet.

Even if you don't offer terms (say, everything you sell online is paid in advance) — you still need a cash flow analysis, and you should go through this exercise to determine if you will have enough cash coming in to pay your expenses.

By adding "Beginning Cash" to "Sales Receipts" you have an estimate of the amount of cash you will have during the month to pay the bills for that month.

In the event this amount is not sufficient to pay your anticipated bills you will have to temporarily borrow enough money to carry you until your available cash increases sufficiently.

Operating Loan

The purpose of the operating loan line item is to show exactly how much money you will need to borrow in order to keep your bills paid. This number is calculated by subtracting "Expenses" (Total Projected Cash Out) from Total Cash Available.

Expenses

The next section is a list of all your categories of expenses that must be paid each month of your forecast. The line items in this section do not have to be as detailed as they are in your pro forma financial statements because many items can be combined — as long as you don't leave out any amounts.

Ending Cash

The last line item then is your calculated "Ending Cash" at the end of each month, which, of course, is automatically the "Beginning Cash" for the following month.

When looking at the sample *Cash Flow Analysis*, you will see that by the second month of the analysis (forecast) you will need to borrow money ("Operating Loan") in order to pay all of your expenses for the next seven months. After that, you have enough cash flow to not only meet your expenses, but you can pay back your operating loan as well.

Note: There are, of course, many ways to accommodate a shortfall as small as the one shown in the above example — but the purpose here is to demonstrate this "system" of cash flow analysis … not any specific numbers.

Updating

It is obvious when you fill out a form such as this, how looking at income and expenses in this kind of detail can give you the best picture of how your cash should flow throughout the ensuing 12 months.

However, a more important activity is to update each month with the *Actual* numbers that occurred that month. Simply overwrite the actual numbers on top of the projected numbers on your spreadsheet.

Remember, this is a system for dealing with "cash flow," and no accruals are allowed.

This step will give you more information for fine-tuning the projections for future months. The more actual months you have to work from, the more accurate your future projections will become.

This particular cash flow analysis system best serves the smaller business. As your business grows, there are other ways to control and analyze your cash flow.

This chapter is certainly not a complete discussion on cash flow analysis. I only included this one small business system for analyzing your cash flow because I said your accountant-prepared *Statement of Cash Flow* was of little use in helping you manage your business.

If you and your accountant agree on some other system for controlling your cash flow, you should most assuredly use that system.

Small Business Accounting Software

Initially, you likely won't need small business accounting software — unless you are going into a bookkeeping service business. To begin with, a simple hand-written sales and expense sheet is all you need for a basic small business accounting system.

You do not need accounting software at the outset for a very small and simple business.

Furthermore, I recommend you outsource your bookkeeping as you grow into a larger operation, because your time is much better utilized in building your business than in doing bookkeeping.

I want to caution you against getting so involved in the technical aspects of your accounting system and software that your daily business operation suffers. Unfortunately, this happens all too often.

Moreover, when you grow large enough to require an on-site bookkeeper, you will want to provide the small business accounting software that they are most familiar with.

However, if your new business has inventory that must be tracked, or you use point of sale data collection, or you need specialized reports at month-end that would be costly to prepare manually … then you will likely need to install some form of small business accounting software that can be utilized by an independent contractor, or part-time bookkeeper.

I'll say again; learn what your financial statements can tell you, and learn what additional information your bookkeeper or accountant can provide you — but don't get caught up in the minutiae of everyday bookkeeping.

At the same time, I know that most of you will not heed this advice, and will only go somewhere else for information on accounting software.

So, if you are searching for an accounting software package for your business, I suggest you check out this URL for a short description of each of the most popular accounting software packages available today. http://www.business-solutions-and-resources.com/accounting-software-for-small-business.html

In the meantime, here is a short list of the most popular software providers from the over 100 small business accounting software packages currently available:

Quickbooks/Quickbooks Pro

This is, without a doubt, the most widely used small business accounting software available to small business today. This is a complete accounting software package (detailed inventory control requires upgrading to the

"Premier" edition), and is the easiest of all packages to set up and use. It also has a Mac version.

Peachtree Accounting by SAGE

This software has been around for some time, and is quite comprehensive and easy to use. There are several different editions of this software available to handle most small businesses, including more advanced bookkeeping.

MYOB Accounting Software

This company provides accounting software for both Windows and Mac. They also have several editors for different levels of complexity in your bookkeeping requirements.

SAGE Business Works Accounting

This is a more comprehensive software package for the larger small business. It has integrated modules and is network capable for multiple users.

Cougar Mountain Software

This is a more complete accounting system where different modules can be purchased according to the needs of your business.

Mamut

This appears to be an excellent accounting software package for the small to medium size business. There are three editions available: startup, standard, and professional.

Free Software

There are also many "free" accounting software packages available — simply Google "free bookkeeping software" and you will have your list. Just note that these packages offer only the bare minimum of capability … but a number of them can be upgraded — for a fee.

I will point out, however, that many accountants complain about the free and low cost small business accounting software packages, because they do not have adequate internal controls built in.

Also, when your business grows to a point where these free software packages are no longer adequate, you may have serious problems converting your company over to more sophisticated and appropriate accounting software.

Whether you set up your own small business accounting software system, or outsource your accounting work … it is strictly up to you. In either case, the necessity to understand your financial statements remains the same.

Complementary Recordkeeping

Complementary recordkeeping is a subject you will not read much about anywhere else, because it is rarely mentioned in classrooms ... and people who have never owned an active small business often ignore it.

In just about every small business, financial statements are not timely enough to help you with your day-to-day operations. That is not the purpose of financial statements anyway.

Financial statements are "reports," they tell you about your past overall performance. What you also need is a system that presents to you what is happening today — preferably this hour.

This is especially true in the early days of your startup. Cash will be at a premium and you don't want to waste a single cent. This is where complementary recordkeeping becomes necessary.

So, how do you best track the daily finances and operations of your small business? This is where you need to be innovative and create your own little "hip-pocket" system for tracking what goes on in your business each day.

If your business is simple and straightforward, say like a coffee cart business for example, there is not much more you need to do beyond the simple daily recordkeeping system of sales and expenses — for your financial records.

At the same time, however, you should be keeping track of which coffees sell best, which pastries sell out first (and which ones don't), plus noting any special requests from customers.

You are in business to make people your loyal customers, so you need to know, as precisely as possible, what pleases them. Recording this information consistently (people's habits change) is the key to running a successful small business.

When businesses are somewhat larger than the coffee cart example, it becomes a little more interesting. You may be able to track things like: daily phone inquiries vs. sales…or daily sales as a major marker for future profitability (depending on discounts given to get the sales)…total hours worked…shipments…mood of your employees…the weather, and/or any other "marker" you can relate to performance of your business.

 Many business owners carry a small spiral notepad around to record these special markers so they can develop and study daily trends and establish norms.

This is not to say you won't need a complete small bookkeeping system — because as your business grows, you will. And you will need your small business financial statements completed in a timely fashion for all the other required analyses.

But to keep your fingers on the pulse of your business — whatever business that is — you need to develop much more timely information on the operation of your business. You need complementary recordkeeping and immediate analysis of the information.

And, either you have to do that yourself (which is what I recommend), or you have to train someone to collect the data and do the analysis for you.

About the Author

My name is Bob Foster and I am a small-business advisor. My background spans a few decades and is unusually eclectic in that it includes working with the smallest of small businesses as well as Fortune 100 companies.

I have worked as CEO or consultant at businesses from the high-tech world of the "Silicon Rain Forest," to the commercial fishing grounds of Alaska and Mexico.

I've worked on projects involving products from beer to computers, and in industries from pulp and paper to urban renewal.

Along the way I earned a reputation for saving businesses that were deemed unsalvageable—and that is what spawned my book *Be Your Own Turnaround Manager*

I started businesses and sold businesses, and was lied to by large multi national corporations (according to the late *Wilson Harrell*, all big corporations lie). As an entrepreneur, I felt the excitement of success as well as the sting of failure.

Even though I spent part of my career working for large corporations, it is the small business arena that excites me—where Entrepreneurs are born and flourish.

So, that is the foundation and background upon which I am now sharing with entrepreneurs everywhere—what I learned from real experiences, not just in classrooms.

My goal is to fan the flames of the entrepreneurial spirit, and to encourage and nurture the entrepreneur in us all.

Good luck, and I wish you much success! —Bob Foster

Contact:
bob@business-solutions-and-resources.com

Website:

http://www.business-solutions-and-resources.com

APPENDIX

Sample Balance Sheet

Sample Profit & Loss Statement

Sample Cash Flow Projections

ABC MANUFACTURING, INC.
Balance Sheet
For Year Ending December 31, 20XX

ASSETS

Current Assets

Cash	10,525
Accounts Receivable	27,000
Inventory	30,000
Prepaid Expenses	2,000
Total Current Assets	69,525

Fixed Assets

Property—net of depreciation	215,000
Equipment—net of depreciation	80,000
Vehicles—net of depreciation	5,000
Total Fixed Assets	300,000
Total Assets	369,525

LIABILITIES

Current Liabilities

Revolving lines of credit	20,000
Accounts Payable	5,000
Current Portion of Long-term Debt	15,000
Total Current Liabilities	40,000

Long-term Liabilities

Long-term debt and capital leases	45,500
Loans payable to stockholders	60,500
Total Long-term Liabilities	106,000
Total Liabilities	146,000

Stockholders Equity

Common stock	1,000
Additional Paid-in Capital	25,000
Retained Earnings (Cum from prior years)	53,190
Retained Earnings (From current P&L)	144,335
Total Stockholders Equity	223,525
Total Liabilities and Stockholders Equity	369,525

ABC MANUFACTURING, INC.
Profit and Loss Statement
Year Ended December 31, 20XX

			%
Sales		1,750,450	
Returns and allowances		2,752	
	Net Sales	1,747,698	100.0
Cost of Sales			
Beginning Inventory		50,000	
Purchases		610,162	
Production Labor		420,108	
Ending Inventory		30,000	
	Total Cost of Sales	1,050,270	60.1
	Gross Profit	697,428	39.9
Selling Expense			
Wages		75,000	
Commissions		25,000	
Marketing		25,000	
	Total Selling Expenses	125,000	7.2
Operating Expense			
Salaries		225,000	
Payroll taxes		29,000	
Benefits		27,000	
Office Supplies		500	
Postage		250	
Professional Fees		2,000	
Telephone		850	
Utilities		950	
Training & Education		250	
Miscellaneous		50	
	Total Operating Expense	285,850	16.4
Operating Profit—EBITDA		286,578	16.4
Other Income (Expense)			
Interest		(9,650)	
Depreciation		(12,000)	
Amortization		(2,500)	
Total Other Income (Expense)		(24,150)	
	Total Pre-tax Profit	262,428	15.0
Income Tax Allowance		118,093	
	Net Profit	144,335	8.3

January 1, 20xx

Cash Flow Analysis--Projections
ABC Manufacturing, Inc.

--Projected Activity--	January	February	March	April	May	June	July	August	September	October	November	December	Total
Beginning Cash	5,000	1,988	9,488	8,163	5,513	1,213	213	1,038	4,013	7,488	11,813	13,163	
Sales:													
Sales Billings (reference only)	4,500	6,000	7,000	8,000	10,000	6,000	5,000	3,000	3,000	5,000	8,000	10,000	75,500
Sales Receipts	2,000	3,000	4,500	3,500	2,500	4,500	6,000	7,500	8,000	9,500	7,500	11,000	69,500
Operating Loan	0	10,000	0	0	0	0	0	0	0	0	0	0	10,000
Total Cash Available	7,000	14,988	13,988	11,663	8,013	5,713	6,213	8,538	12,013	16,988	19,313	24,163	
Expenses:													
Materials	900	1,200	1,400	1,600	2,000	1,200	1,000	600	600	1,000	1,600	2,000	15,100
Payroll	3,000	3,000	3,000	3,000	3,000	3,000	3,000	3,000	3,000	3,000	3,000	3,000	36,000
Advertising	225	300	350	400	500	300	250	150	150	250	400	500	3,775
Commissions	338	450	525	600	750	450	375	225	225	375	600	750	5,663
Office Supplies	50	50	50	50	50	50	50	50	50	50	50	50	600
All Other Costs	500	500	500	500	500	500	500	500	500	500	500	500	6,000
(You can list more here)													
Total Projected Cash Out	5,013	5,500	5,825	6,150	6,800	5,500	5,175	4,525	4,525	5,175	6,150	6,800	67,138
Ending Cash	1,988	9,488	8,163	5,513	1,213	213	1,038	4,013	7,488	11,813	13,163	17,363	

Assumptions:

(1) That ABC Manufacturing offers payment terms on all of its billings.

(2) That ABC Manufacturing has enough historical data, or experience, to make accurate sales & expense projections.

Instructions:

Use this example as a guide to develop your own spread sheet for analyzing your potential cash flow.

Sales Billings are shown only as a guide for calculating Cash Receipts--depending on your businesses history, or forecasts.

Note that in this example, ABC will have to borrow an additional $10,000 to not run out of money during this time period.

Printed in Great Britain
by Amazon.co.uk, Ltd.,
Marston Gate.